D1249573

WILLIAM, THE WHAT-IF WONDER ON HIS FIRST DAY OF SCHOOL

Written by Carol Wulff, LSW

Contributions by Margaret R. Mauzé, PhD, ABPP
Board Certified Pediatric Psychologist

Illustrations by Clare Willett

IT'S A WONDER PUBLISHING, LLC

For permission requests, contact the author at
carol@thewhatifwonder.com

Cover and Interior Book Design by
Alex Lucas at Oh The Raven Studio
www.ohtheraven.com

Cover and Interior Book Illustrations by
Clare Willett

DISCLAIMERS:
The author does not intend for this book to be a substitute for medical advice of physicians. The reader should regularly consult a physician in matters relating to their health and particularly with respect to any symptoms that may require diagnosis or medical attention.

Names and persons in this book are entirely fictional. They bear no resemblance to anyone living or deceased.

ISBN 978-0-692-06568-6

IT'S A WONDER PUBLISHING, LLC

It's A Wonder Publishing, LLC
PO Box 99
Bath, OH 44210-9800

"This book is a great age- and developmentally appropriate way to teach children how to manage their 'worry thoughts.' The book is designed around a common situation that most children, and adults, can identify with, and can then use the simplicity of the strategy to generalize to other situations. The information at the end is very helpful, as well."

—Kate Eshleman, PsyD
Pediatric Psychologist
Cleveland, Ohio

"As a pediatrician in private practice for over 18 years, I estimate that at least half of the visits I see each day relate directly or indirectly to anxiety in my patients or their parents. This book is a beautifully illustrated, wonderful tool to help parents assist their child to navigate through their anxieties (or the what-ifs). As a parent I am familiar with the what-ifs. I would have loved to have this children's book years ago."

—John T. Fitch Jr., MD, FAAP
Heritage Pediatrics
San Antonio, Texas

To all those with butterflies in their bellies who feel nervous and scared with each new situation. May you become the next What-If Wonder!

To Dan, Michael, Natalie, and Allison—XO

—CAROL

To all the children and families who trust me to walk this journey with them. Your strength and power inspire me every day. And to my own wonderful family, with love.

—MARA

To all the people who saw past my what-ifs and saw the wonder I could do.

—CLARE

PREFACE

William, the What-If Wonder is a story of a young boy struggling to conquer his fear and anxiety about the first day of school and all the changes that entails. On every page, the story stresses the use of cognitive reframing to help learn to recognize worry versus reality. Cognitive reframing is a psychological technique for looking at the same situation in a different way.

Throughout the story, each first-day-of-school what-if worry is countered with a more likely outcome. By recognizing the more likely outcomes, William realizes he has the power within to conquer his pestering what-if thoughts and manage his anxiety more effectively.

A Note to Parents and Caregivers section at the end of the book, written by Margaret R. Mauzé, PhD, ABPP, gives more information on teaching children ways to manage their anxiety.

Hello! I'm William, as you can see!
The first day of school will be hard for me.

Worried and scared as I roll out of bed,
so many what-ifs are inside my head!

They cause me to see what might not be true,

but I have the power to see a new view!

What if the bus passes right by my street?

Look! The door opened. Now I'll find a seat.

What if I trip and they laugh in my face?

"Sit here next to me—in this open space."

What if we're lost and we can't find the school?

Wow! That was fast! And this place is so cool!

What if my tears start to run down my cheek?

"No need to be sad. We'll have a great week!"

What if in class all the desks look the same?

Mine's easy to find. See, there is my name!

What if my lunch isn't served like they say?

"When you're done with lunch, we'll go out
and play."

What if I'm hurt and I need someone's care?

There are people to help me everywhere!

What if my teacher would leave me behind?

"Follow me, class, in a straight, single line!"

What if I can't find the potty at all?

"Class, there's the restroom. It's right down the hall!"

What if the bus leaves without me for home?

The bus driver's here! I'm never alone.

I'm the What-If Wonder. What a great day!

With my power I pushed all those what-ifs away!

NOTE TO PARENTS & CAREGIVERS

Margaret R. Mauzé, PhD, ABPP

If you are the parent or caregiver of an anxious child, you know how it feels to face a barrage of questions from your child when they go to a new place or face a change in routine. You know the frustration and exhaustion that come from ineffectively trying to reassure and comfort your child. Your child also knows these challenges. Children with anxiety can experience an endless flood of worry that they find difficult to control. Worry impacts how they feel and how they think, causing a rush of physical reactions like fast breathing, butterflies in their stomach, and sweaty palms, as well as anxious thoughts they can't seem to control.

The ability to manage these reactions is largely a learned skill, and parents as well as caregivers play a crucial role in teaching children ways to manage their anxiety. This job can become challenging, as parents and caregivers may struggle themselves with anxiety, or may become frustrated and distressed when trying to help their children.

William, the What-If Wonder on His First Day of School is designed to help both parents and children learn to combat the worries that children can find unrelenting. Based on the principles of cognitive reframing, William verbalizes his anxious what-if thoughts, as well as counter thoughts that help him find alternatives to his anxious ones. This helps children learn to "boss" back their worry and take control over their anxious thoughts. When you read this book with your child, you can enhance its benefits in a variety of ways:

• Read the book aloud, taking your time. The rhyming may help younger children commit the principles to memory and make reading enjoyable for parents and children alike.

• Empathize with William's anxiety when he faces a new situation. "It can be hard to get on the bus and not know who to sit with, but look, another child asks him to sit down." You provide understanding to your child while also helping them see alternative possibilities.

• Ask your child what other things William could say to himself to counteract anxious thoughts. "He's nervous about getting lost. What would you say to him to make him feel better?" This helps your child begin to form their own ideas about counter thoughts.

• Ask your child if they have ever felt the way William has, and what they do to feel better. Then talk about additional things your child can do to feel better. Also encourage your child to find ways to calm down when feeling physical signs of anxiety. "I take ten slow, deep breaths when I have butterflies in my tummy."

• Reference *William, the What-If Wonder* at other times during your child's day. For example, if your child is nervous about an event or activity, ask your child what William would do or say in the same situation.

Using these techniques can help your child to view their anxiety as a separate entity with its own identity. This can help them "boss" back the anxiety and feel more capable of taking control over it. Some children may want to create their own superhero persona that helps them feel they can combat their anxiety. Encourage them to use their imagination and these skills to gain control over their anxiety.

If your child's anxiety seems out of proportion to the situation they are in, or if your child's anxiety is significantly interfering with their life (keeping them from social activities, hurting school attendance, disrupting sleep), please consult with a therapist who can work with you and your child to find more techniques to manage the anxiety. If you think you or your child may need to meet with a therapist, your pediatrician may be a good resource for referral information.

BIOGRAPHY

Carol Wulff, LSW, is a Licensed Social Worker and mother of a child with anxiety. Remembering how painful it was to witness her child's mind racing just to get through the simplest of tasks, she vowed to one day write a book to help others learn how to tackle those annoying what-if thoughts. Cognitive reframing—seeing the same situation in a new way—empowered her child to manage the anxiety and approach new situations with confidence. She created the William, the What-If Wonder book series to help children learn how to use their power to change their view and see past their worrisome thoughts. Carol lives in Medina, Ohio, with her husband and three children.

Margaret R. Mauzé, PhD, ABPP, is a board certified pediatric psychologist. She earned her PhD in clinical child and adolescent psychology from the University of Kansas in 2005. She achieved specialty board certification from the American Board of Professional Psychology in the area of clinical child and adolescent psychology in 2008. She worked at Cleveland Clinic Children's Hospital for seven years before moving into private practice. She has special interest in working with children with acute and chronic medical illness and children struggling with anxiety and depression. She currently lives in San Antonio, Texas, with her husband and two children.

Clare Willett enjoys creating characters and bringing them to life! She has created city logos and enjoys sharing her artistic talents when needed. She is pursuing a career in zoology and wildlife management.

William, The What-If Wonder Book Series

The William, the What-If Wonder book series is designed to help children with anxiety learn how to navigate their worries when faced with the uncertainty of new situations. Every story focuses on a common childhood experience that may be overwhelming to a child with anxiety and begins to teach the child ways to manage that anxiety. William struggles with many anxious thoughts that dominate his day, but he uses different strategies such as problem solving and cognitive reframing to see these situations in a new way. These strategies remind him he has the power to find positive solutions to his perceived problems.

By following William's journey, children and families can learn useful strategies to conquer their own anxiety and take control over their anxious thoughts. A Note to Parents and Caregivers section, written by a board certified pediatric psychologist, is at the back of each book to further help children and families generalize these strategies to their own lives.

Book #1: *William, the What-If Wonder on His First Day of School*
Book #2: *William, the What-If Wonder and His Sleepover Worries*

CPSIA information can be obtained
at www.ICGtesting.com
Printed in the USA
BVHW021940290721
613187BV00002B/99